SEEDS OF HOPE

Rochinda Pickens

Co-Authors

Delano Berry

Roscheeta Brundige

Trea Coleman

Brandi Copeland

Marla Henderson

Clarissa Knighten

Nia Taylor

Purpose Publishing
1503 Main Street
Grandview, MO 64030

Seeds of Hope
Copyright © 2021 by Rochinda Pickens

ISBN: 9798749515633

Cover Design: Ejuan Henderson
Edited by Cheryl Richardson

For permission requests, write to the author at the email address below.

Bulk Ordering Information: Quantity sales. Special discounts are available on quantity purchases by churches, ministry associations, and others. Contact the ChindaandFriends.com website for details.

For speaking engagements, interviews or more information, contact the author at ChindaandFriends@gmail.com

Printed in the Unites States of America

DEDICATION

To my amazing Lord and Savior Jesus Christ, thank you for the Seeds of Hope. I dedicate this book to my mother Josephine Ann Berry-Hooks, the root of my life and the most important seed that God allowed me to have. The conception of this book was manifested through our countless conversations. You reminded me daily that seeds of hope are to be shared with the world. You told me to always stay rooted in my faith and never loose "HOPE". As I began writing my chapter I remember you asking me how could you be a part of the anthology. My response was, Mama you are the root to my being and you will be in the book forever. Mama was looking forward to being a part of this book. Everyday, when she remembered, she would ask, & How's the book coming along? She reminded me that she would need some help wit finishing her chapter as she recolected her thoughts.

November 24th, 2020 my amazing seed of hope took flight into heaven unexpectedly. Your legacy was left in your children, grandchildren and great-great grandchildren. Mama, your seeds of hope have BLOOMED and Blossomed I love and miss you. Love, Your Daughter, Rochinda

FOREWORD

Everything always happens for a reason. In the best of times, the worst of times, and everything in between. Of course, we may not always understand why certain things happen to us or why we sometimes experience emotional pain, physical illness, loss of a loved one, or other kinds of trauma, the fact still remains…everything really does happen for a reason.

I was actually taught this particular truth at a very young age, but I will admit, that it wasn't until I became an adult that I was truly able to confirm it. It wasn't until I found myself pondering my overall life experiences and thinking hard about how I got from point A to point B that I came to realize just how perfectly God had planned out my destiny. For example, when I was a child, even though I didn't think I would ever have any real use for the typing classes my mom encouraged me to take both in high school and at our community college, little did I know that, eventually, the day would come when I would be passed over for more than one corporate job promotion and that even with as hurt and disappointed as I was, God would soon place it on my heart to sit down and begin writing my first book. I certainly had no idea that I would go on to write twenty-seven more of them, and that each and every one of those manuscripts I wrote would require me to write thousands upon thousands of words. And just imagine how much longer it would have taken me to write those books with pen and paper. I mean who would have guessed that something as normal as taking a few advanced typing courses would set the stage for part of the purpose that God had assigned to my life, well before I even considered the idea of writing a book?

Then there were some of the more painful moments in my life that became wonderful testimonies for me, such as my being touched inappropriately between the ages of six and eleven years old...my being hurt and betrayed by some friends and family members whom I'd loved and trusted for years...and my losing my dear, sweet mom when she was only fifty-seven years old. Because thankfully, what I can tell you today is that all the heartache and grief I endured is what made me stronger, wiser, and more determined than ever to keep going. Those unfortunate moments in my life ultimately turned into seeds of hope and showed me just how powerful and true Jeremiah 29:11 actually is: "For I know the plans I have for you," declares the LORD, "plans to prosper you and not to harm you, plans to give you hope and a future."

This is also the reason I am honored to introduce to you, Seeds of Hope, where Rochinda Pickens, along with her seven coauthors have written the kind of powerful, inspirational, and spirit-filled stories that will have you reflecting about your own life experiences. These thought-provoking messages will inspire and empower you, and best of all, you will be blessed by each author's divine revelation and noticeable transparency. You will discover, beyond a shadow of a doubt, that the most important thing we can ever do for ourselves is to trust and depend on God at all times...and to never give up under any circumstances.

Kimberla Lawson Roby
New York Times Bestselling Author,
Speaker, and Podcast Host
www.kimroby.com

INTRODUCTION

H uman life begins when a seed is planted, nurtured, and protected. That seed will bloom into a human being that will be shaped by experiences. Those experiences are more than events, people, places, and things. Instead, each experience represents a new seed entering our journey that will be planted and watered or passed on. No matter how far we go in life, there will always be a point where we are called to reflect on our past to assess our beginning.

The Seeds of Hope will take readers on eight amazing journeys through reflections on soul-shaping moments brought about by seeds long since planted, ripened, and ready for harvest. There will be seeds that were intentionally incorporated while heading to a specific destination or those of divine purpose, reason, and season. In all, The Seeds of Hope will add context to the complexities of spiritual growth.

By inviting readers to the challenge of identifying their seeds, The Seeds of Hope becomes a useful resource to create your own sacred space to commune, explore, practically apply, and rise. God made us all in His image and He is multifaceted; just as each soul who begins their journey as a seed.

I am the daughter of Josephne Ann Hooks and Charles Berry; the grandaughter of Zepher Ann Hooks and Gus Kerr. My mother retired from the City of Kansas City and my father was self-employed. From their seed of hope; they produced life.

Join Rochinda Pickens and co-authors as they invite you into the many facets, trials, and tribulations proving there is no story void of God's glory.

TABLE OF CONTENTS

ROOTED

ROCHINDA PICKENS

On the surface, a seed seems simple. However, a seed is a reproductive structure that disperses and can survive over time due to three basic parts: an embryo, a nutrient supply, and a protective coating. I always knew that a seed was the shell housing an extension of life to be grown. I knew seeds had to be fed and nurtured for that life to take form. At one point in my life, that's all I knew and all I thought I needed to know about a seed. My thought process stayed at the surface; plant, feed, nurture, grow. However, life would reveal how the simplest of gifts are much more complex, revealing, and renewing than I ever thought was possible.

Nothing is more beautiful to watch on a windy summer day than the seeds of a particular dandelion flower. We used to call them cotton flowers because they looked like beautiful hollow cotton mounds in the grass among all the other weeds and wildflowers. The simplistic beauty of the seemingly weightless, perfectly round, mound of individual seeds clinging to the head of the flower, is fascinating. The real show begins when the wind blows with enough speed to detach the individual stems of cotton from the head of the flower.

Those seeds take flight! In no time the air would be filled with cotton stems light enough to dance in the wind but with just enough weight to find a new destination. You see, just because a seed is planted doesn't mean it's stationary. That seed will not only become life but eventually, take on a new life. It took time and life experience to understand and to see how this had already been true in my life. When I was growing up, there were eight seeds in the home, myself, my siblings, and my mother. We all lived life as a family while living out our experiences as individuals within that family.

In time, I learned that each person, seed, in my family represented a valuable attribute. I witnessed these seeds becoming better versions of themselves over time in the most impactful ways. I witnessed how the weight of life can sharpen and perfect perseverance. I marveled at how loss awakened keen wisdom. I was inspired by how inconsistencies in the world fostered an unwavering strength that became unshakable. I prayed to know how to possess the spirit and mind to have the fight in me I watched firsthand. And I never forgot the energy in the air when space is shared with a true survivor. I never knew the shell of a seed housed this much-but God! At this season in my life, this time of reflecting, God wanted me to know and understand the depth of seeds in my life. As always, truth and thorough understanding begin at the root. My mother, the root of our life, was the most important seed of all – hope. When I began exploring my root, I began the journey of understanding my life as a multitude of seeds.

The Origin of Our Seeds

Everything has a beginning, a root. If you imagine any root in nature, there are always extensions on that root. Just the same, the instructions within a seed are vast. We can see this in all of the details of the harvest. This is why the beginning of any story is so important. Taking the trip back to my root, hope, made the challenges I've faced, the choices I've made, and the outcomes a little more clear. Arriving at a space where I connected to my reality of living and growing on a foundation of hope, a context was created for how I saw the world. With my context came a couple of lessons: appreciate the unique growth of my seed and own that unique growth.

Appreciating, Owning, Elevating

There is so much power and glory in a story when you're all in. Still, the truth is being "all in" is a work that requires constant practice. It would have been great if I had stepped into my adult years crystal clear about who I was and had walked as her through life. I didn't know how to appreciate how I was uniquely made because I had no real sense of the glory in my making. I didn't see the awkwardness and insecurities as a part of a creation that was significant. When I imagined the best version of myself, it was like imagining the perfect man for me-it was a fantasy. Fantasies of the flesh are free from the same flaws God uses to perfect His creation in his image. I had no connection to the beauty of uniquely flawed seeds because I had no connection to the gifts of my flaws and His design in choosing those flaws for me. God always knew who I was and what my seed would mature to be. God always knew my journey and the flaws necessary to refine my soul for His mission.

Every inch of me from the ends of the hair on my head to the tips of my toenails, the flawless to the flawed, was His intentional design for me. Then, and only then could I appreciate my unique differences. Appreciation leads to owning or being able to unapologetically sit in every facet of my seeds. This is important because seeds will be dropped within us and along our paths throughout life. When we understand our roots, appreciate our unique seeds, and are comfortable with the good, bad, and indifferent, in owning our unique journey, the tools we need along the way will be God's never ending gift.

The Transformation of a Seed

I used to dream of being on the cover of fashion magazines. My tall slender frame and my eye for fabric and color were what the industry needed. For years I flipped through the pages of my favorite magazines and made sure to make every day my runway show. It's funny how God can take what we imagine and tweak it for His purpose. It turned out that the vision I had for myself on the cover of magazines was an extension of His plan for me. I wouldn't grace a cover until I cultivated the soil of my life and my seeds. What does this mean? This means that I needed to learn what it took to make it to a magazine cover. There's more to a cover than a pretty photo. You are considered to be the center of a cover story when you have done something worth sharing with others. As I lived my life, I came to understand that the soil of my life was cultivated to hold seeds of service. Service to others while connecting people became the center of my existence. Before I knew it, flipping through those fashion magazines for style inspiration for my cover story took on new meaning.

When we cultivate the soil of our lives by laying out the foundation for our vision and living in that truth we open ourselves up. We leave a crack in the door for God to show us His version, the spiritual version, of the image we have of ourselves in this flesh. I eventually made that cover and the story worth sharing was me connecting women and describing to readers "The Life I Love". Because God loves me and rewards obedience, I was able to showcase my fashion sense as well! It was God's plan for my vision as a model for clothing to be traded for His vision of an influencer connecting women to glorify their journeys in Christ while modeling clothes on that cover.

The point here is we have a limited understanding of what we want and what we believe is important. What is important for us in service to God for others is a different matter. Remaining open to the twists and turns of your pathway while moving in faith with obedience is how His glory can manifest and amplify your vision. Your vision is made of many different seeds all growing in their own time. Never let what you see rush nature's timeframe for harvest.

Our Life Experiences Are For Others

As I write I think about how this is just the beginning of what God has in store for those I serve. This means there is much more to come from me. I would be untruthful if I said I'm not curious about the next twist or turn God has in store. Already, God is changing the way He works through me and it is an exciting journey. Sometimes it's a lot but I love what I do and I'm always waiting to receive the next assignment. In all, there is fruit to be harvested from my seeds and this fruit isn't to be set in a pretty bowl on my table. This fruit is to be packaged up and dropped off on the doorstep of many. New seeds are being planted daily and soon that fruit will need to be harvested and shared as well. This is a process for all of us.

Our harvest is for others. The worst thing we can do is keep that fruit for ourselves. God has shown me that no matter what, I am covered when I cover others. With an open hand and open heart, I live to own the truth of His word. My hope for anyone who reads this anthology is that you are compelled to examine the root of your life, own your uniqueness without comparing your differences, cultivate the soil of your life for the seeds of your vision, and share your fruits freely.

Reflection:

You are not reading this book by accident. You are holding this book on purpose and for a divine purpose so let me challenge you to go a little further. I challenge you to dig deep and determine if there are seeds of hope within you that are ready to be awakened and join you on your journey.

Beginning to explore your seeds may seem like a heavy task but it's easier than you may think. My advice would be to find a quiet space where you can connect to changes that have elevated you; ones you may not be able to explain.

Also, look to challenges that continue to reappear. Finally, refocus on your prayers. Have you created a consistent place to receive answers? This process begins with you but God intends to expand and impact others. Exploring seeds within and distributing them globally to others is an ongoing work through Kept Woman of God Ministry (501c (3) organization).

Our growth is to be realized and our mission shared to uplift and elevate others. Please consider sowing a monthly seed of $10 or more to support our organization. Join us at www.keptwomanofgod.com to make automatic monthly contributions or a one time gift. We truly appreciate your love, support, and willingness to grow with us.

Blessings and Abundance,

Rochinda

Rochinda Pickens

Rochinda Pickens is a life shift coach, motivational speaker and best-selling author. She has a passion for helping women who have made the empowering decision to live again! These amazing women are embracing their breakdowns while preparing for their breakthroughs. After surviving a fatal car accident, that changed the life of this mother of three. She was forced to make some difficult decisions, one being moving on, after having her life, literally broken down. Without a college degree or any formal training, the thing successful entrepreneurs are assumed to possess. She successfully owned and operated Chinda's Younique Boutique for 10 years.

During this time, she was honored to meet amazing women from all walks of life. She also discovered that one of God's callings for her life was to show women what intentional living looks like. With a renewed zest for life while discovering the passion experienced from sharing her story and helping other women. She started Kept Woman of God (KWOG) a 501c3 nonprofit organization that connects with women globally through conferences, workshops and retreats. These experiences allow women to be their authentic selves. Additionally, men and women can share their voices and stress through participating in her book collaborations with God's guidance Rochinda has broken through the barriers and has a passion for passing along what she has learned to others, of starting over and equipping others. She has added a new company, Chinda and Friends, to her list of accomplishments. As well, an eCommerce busness dealing with clean living. Always wanting to be a source of hope to others, her company motto is, "Everyone who enters the door - come in as friends, but hang around long enough, and you become family." Her signature talk is Finding Joy in the Journey: Choosing to Live Intentionally.

Rochinda is a member of the Sister Circle of Greater Kansas City, a three-time national best-selling author. She has created a program, Write with Chinda, that has helped women and men share their stories and become published authors. Her famous phrase is: "It's not a minute, moment or weekend. It's a lifestyle."

BRANDI COPELAND

Journey In The Sun To The Son:
In the Purposed Ground

I n the spring of 2012, I found myself barreling over the toilet in unimaginable grief. This incident led to me being forcefully admitted into the hospital due to my body being riddled with illness. Stress related psoriasis covered my legs, chest and arms. My hair was falling out, and my blood pressure skyrocketed to the point I temporarily lost my vision. I am unable to pinpoint just one thing to attribute this sickness to; was it the heart wrenching pain of giving my heart once again and giving my all to the unlovely, unworthy and undeserving? Was it the unexpected loss of promotion and pay? Was it the tumultuous relationship with my mother that led to a spirit of rejection which led to a deeply rooted fear of failure and success? Whatever it was, I knew I was falling apart, dying slowly inside. Despite the number of things I could attribute my illness to, one thing I knew for sure, there had to be more to life. My children deserved a better version of me. There was a need, no, a heart wrenching, soul bearing plea for a drastic change! It was as if the Lord was speaking to me, as he'd once spoken to the children of Israel, "You have stayed at this mountain long enough."

Committed to change, I applied for positions in every state that had an opening. I was willing to make a lateral career move just to find solace and balance in my physical, mental, emotional, and spiritual life. Unbeknownst to me, God was working in the background or should I say the "purposed" ground for me to make that move and one even greater move that required a bold walk of faith. It was the first step to a more intimate relationship with Him and Him alone. Within two months, I was offered, without an interview, a position in Tampa, Florida. So, with a prayer for protection I jumped at the chance to experience all the opportunities God had for me.

On June 23, 2012, my daughters, my youngest brother and I put Kansas City in the rearview and began our relocation to the Sunshine State. The position offered no relocation expenses so I needed to save all the money I could. My Honda Civic, gave great gas mileage on the winding mountain roads and as a result, I reached 500+ miles per tank. I was so shocked, that I took a picture; needless to say, with it only being nearly a 1300-mile drive, I paid less than $125 for the gas. I actually paid more for the U-Haul than gas for the entire trip! It was a testimony of how during this God-orchestrated journey to Florida God showed me that He can and He will provide!

We moved to Clearwater Florida in the middle of Tropical Storm Debby. While everyone was trying to get out, we were moving in. I did not really understand tropical storms or hurricanes at the time. As we were driving there, we could see the devastation in the hotels we stayed in and the surrounding area. FEMA was on the ground and occupying some of the hotel rooms. The effects of the devastation were defined by the water lines on the walls. Some of the rooms we stayed in reeked of dampness, the presence of mold surrounded the windows, the squishing sounds of water rang in our ears, our shoes soaked, and since the water could not completely be eradicated, the threat of flooding was still imminent. We were not staying there! After an intense search, the hotel staff found us a different room and despite my limited funds, we were willing to pay any cost.

When we finally arrived at my apartment complex in Clearwater, the picture of destruction was similar; flooded apartments, presence of mold and a stench that made your nostrils burn. My apartment complex wasn't the picture-perfect place I had imagined it would be in sunny Florida. Maintenance staff was so busy with water and mold extraction they couldn't come and complete the minor repairs needed in my apartment. The complex lost six maintenance persons within the first few months of our arrival due to the overwhelming amount of work, lack of expertise and lack of adequate pay. I later learned, I'm not sure I wanted them to do the work lacking expertise. In addition, despite needing cosmetic repairs, I found out that my apartment was one of the few that wasn't flooded when the storm hit.

If that was not enough to alarm you, Florida is widely known for its alligators. Not like the Missouri bear, where you only see him in zoos and on the state seal, they are everywhere... literally! Alligators are on display at the zoo, alligators are on display at Busch Gardens, there are "Beware of the Alligators" signs in the public parks. And if that wasn't enough to freak out this transplant, you can feed them their choice delicacy of hot dogs while waiting your turn to play miniature golf! On top of that, you are sure to be graced by the presence of geckos and palmetto bugs in your Floridian welcome packet. However, there is a blessing in having geckos living in and sometimes running across your apartment walls, they ate the bugs and because of the family or generation of geckos living inside of my walls, I did not have the problem that some of my neighbors had with bug infestations. What I gleaned most from this experience is that God put his hedge of protection around us in that move and around our apartment before we arrived and there was even a blessing in the geckos.

He was never meant to stay

When God told Abram to move, he told him to "Leave your country, your people and forefather's households to the land I will show you" (Genesis 12:1, NET) he never meant for him to take his nephew who later caused him more trouble than necessary. Not so with my brother Stephen, although he was never meant to stay there. He helped me with everything. It was the first time I realized I needed help from someone. If I'm honest, I wanted my brother to stay longer than the short time we'd agreed to, at least until my daughters went to school, but God didn't want me to get used to my brother taking care of things. He was preparing me to depend on Him and Him alone. It was the first time I realized I had made a major decision to step out on faith and move away from family, friends and comfort zone, possibly jeopardizing the safety of my daughters in the process.

My brother did have a purpose for being in Florida. On nights when I was sleeping, my brother met with my next-door neighbors. Their friendship became so close that those neighbors looked after me and my children the entire time we lived there. At one point the neighbors had planned to move but stayed because of us. Hebrews 13:2 says "Do not neglect to show hospitality to strangers, for by so doing some people have entertained angels without knowing it." (NIV) Those neighbors were angels in disguise to my family. I tried to repay them for their kindness, but while I was working, they slowly moved out and we never saw each other again.

The kindness of the crossing guard

Jennifer's school was three blocks north and Jackie's school was three blocks south of our apartment. While Jennifer was dropped off at the YMCA for before and after care, Jackie had to walk three blocks to school, sometimes in torrential rains. Not knowing the neighborhood, I could only pray that short walk being on a busy street would be what was needed to protect my daughter from the melting pot state. What I received was greater and God ordained!

Across from the entrance of my apartment, at the corner of Belcher was a crossing guard. The elderly gentleman was both friendly and protective. Each day he watched over my daughter and other students to ensure they crossed the street safely, but he was more than that. When we went to take him a gift when Jackie was returning to Kansas City due to recurring illness, he shared that he watched over her every day, including but not limited to wondering where she was when she didn't come to school on days she was sick. He shared that he never saw her rowdy like the other kids, and it was something about her smile and the fact that she spoke to him daily that made him want to ensure she was okay. He also revealed that he was supposed to retire but decided to stay one more year.

Let's explore our new home...

OMG, while in sunny Florida, we put nearly 5000 miles on my car just to explore as many beaches, parks, malls and whatever entertainment we could afford. The plethora of experiences in Florida was exhilarating and you could spend a lifetime in the state and not touch the surface of what it has to offer. In the winter, the tourists come in droves, but true Floridians leave to get away from the hustle and bustle of the crowds. To them Florida is home, to transplants, it's both home and vacation destination. The twenty minutes of daily rain was nothing compared to the presence and warmth of sun rays. I was more than excited to be there; it was exactly what I needed.

We joined the gym and within 45 days, I lost fifteen pounds. But what I lost most, was the weight of the world upon my shoulders, the presence of stress from the unlovely and the pain of heartbreak from giving too much of my time to the undeserving. I was regaining myself and I was learning that I could depend on God even when I had no one else to depend on. As I spent time journaling my experiences, I met him face to face, not physically as I would stand before you today, but I met his presence, his protection, his guidance, his overwhelming, unfailing, all consuming, far reaching, infinite LOVE.

Psalm 30:11 says "You have changed my sobbing into dancing. You have removed my sackcloth and clothed me with joy." The turnaround journey was not immediate, it was a subtle change of events that led to a realization of the favor of God upon my life. Layer by layer, God was transforming my pain into healing, my tears into joy. Maybe it was the first time I noticed the never-ending smile, maybe it was the Floridian glow, maybe it was when

I no longer felt the heart-wrenching sting of rejection. I do not remember the day when I heard the shackles crashing, but the weight of the world, the insecurities, the fear of failure and success had dissipated and a new and better me was beginning to emerge.

After months of visiting, we settled in at Bible Based Fellowship Church in Tampa, Florida where we were being filled and the church overflowed with "passionate worship, pragmatic preaching and practical Bible study." (Bible Based Fellowship – Our Church, https://www.bible-based.org/our-church/ 02/06/20). At "The Base", as the church was lovingly referred to, my oldest daughter began to mime dance, where she said she felt the power of the Holy Spirit overtake her through dance. My younger daughter joined the choir; a place where she could sing beautiful praises unto the Lord and me, I found a women's ministry actually committed to the spiritual growth of women, a culinary ministry that welcomed my service, and a pastor who was ingrained in the community with his passion for social and community issues. The church kept me grounded during times I felt I was alone, they provided more than just fellowship, they provided a family and I was honored to serve wholeheartedly.

Eight months after I moved my family to Florida, our office received word that the Tampa office was potentially closing. Back home in Kansas City for spring break, I received a call from a coworker stating the rumor was just made official. My life was propelled into a hurricane of emotions and my faith was tested like never before. I want to say that I trusted God to provide a solution, to calm the fears and anxiety I was experiencing; but once again, I ended up in the hospital due to high blood pressure over worry of the outcome.

Fretful, I filed for a hardship transfer and another position in Kansas City in case the hardship transfer fell through. I was offered both; however, God was still working in the midst of my situation despite my lack of faith; making plans for the hardship, I received a phone call from my immediate supervisor that I would be able to return to Kansas City and not be required to move to Jacksonville, Florida like the rest of my department. In addition, the position I accepted to return home was put on hold as the federal government went on a nearly four-week shutdown, so the offer to move immediately was off the table.

The closing of the Tampa office was different from the transformation of the department; our office would close and we were required to report to the Jacksonville office. Riddled with emotional pain and in a constant state of confusion, in anguish of soul, I turned to my church family as they helped me grapple with grief with the tragic loss of a coworker. They helped me weather the storm of the process that bonded thirteen lone staff members whose lives were held in the balance and whose emotions tilted like a car of the steepest roller coaster. It was the strength of support I needed to continue this turnaround journey. The loss of my coworker opened the door to moving to Kansas City, all expenses paid. The job not only paid for a house hunting trip back home, but they packed my home, paid all relocation fees and provided a stipend which allowed us to return home with little or no expense. In addition, I was given a housing allowance to purchase the home I now reside in. Had I followed my own way; I would have missed out on the blessings God provided for me.

In short, I expected a magical experience at Disney, in the warmth and rays of the "sun" Florida offered, a break away from the life I was living that was rooted in pain, a fresh start. What I found in the sun was an encounter with the SON, whom I met face to face. And though I went to every beach and attraction Florida offered that my finances could take my girls and me, the most magical experience was a surrendered heart and a willing spirit that kneeled before his altar in complete and total surrender to his will, his plans and his way! I experienced an intimacy with my heavenly Father that words cannot express. In Florida it was where I learned to depend on God because he was all I had, but he was also all I needed.

Returning home to Kansas City has been a blessing as God allowed me to watch and participate in raising my grandson, reconnecting with my support system of family and friends, reconciling broken friendships and relationships and to be in Kansas City when my mother first collapsed and eventually passed away. My story is to give you courage; a seed of hope to step out on faith even when you can't see your way ahead. To trust God and expect His purposed ground for your life. In addition, don't be afraid make the hard decisions to heal and to move on, to make the sacrifices to keep you emotionally healthy and to do the things that are best for your children without regret. Broken people break people, healed people tell their stories so others can be healed; believers stand in faith and believe that God heals, God cleanses, God delivers and God redeems. Finally, there's purpose in pain.

Brandi Copeland

After learning to internalize her feelings of rejection most of her life, Brandi was overcome by countless health issues due to a tumultuous relationship with her mother, failed relationships, loss of financial security, and improper balance in her personal life. As a result, Brandi suffered from a myriad of health issues such as stress related psoriasis, numerous hospital stays due to high blood pressure and suffered from migraines so intense, she temporarily lost her vision.

In 2012, Brandi followed the voice of God, stepped out on unwavering faith and made the bold decision to move with her two daughters 1200 miles away from family and friends to Clearwater Florida; a place she'd never been but a place she not only found solace in the sun, but where she attributes to meeting the "Son" face to face.

Brandi is proud to co-author The Seeds of Hope. She is currently documenting her lifelong journey of how she is overcoming the obstacles of rejection, learning to continue to increase her faith and how she is unequivocally, unreservedly and unashamedly saying "YES to God.

She holds a Master's degree in Human Services and is currently a Branch Chief at the U.S. Department of HUD, Brandi served four years as the director of her church singles ministry, and presently serves as an usher and Sunday school teacher. She also served as an AmeriCorps VISTA. She is a mother of three and grandmother of one. She continues to motivate men, women and children through her ministry gifts of helps; exhortation and teaching.

WITNESS

Delano Berry

My older brother wasn't the older brother I should look up to and still, I did. From an early age, Joe was a problem child. He did things that were beyond the normal stuff boys would do. He spent our childhood in and out of juvenile detention centers until he aged out and made the transition into adult jails and eventually prison. I stood excited waiting for Joe on one of the visitation days my mother arranged. As I watched him walking toward us, he was larger than life to me. He looked unshakable and fearless only to tell me "Delano, don't be like me. This is no place you want to be".

Although I was the middle child, when I was a boy I took pride in being the protector for my mother and sisters. My dad wasn't around and although I had my older brother Joe, I knew I had to be the one to take care of everyone. I knew a time would come when everything would fall on me so I decided, why wait? If I'm always ready, I'll always be ready. I was thirteen, cocky and sure on the outside. Inside, I would learn later on in life, was a different story. I had mixed feelings about not having my dad around but at least I had Joe.

I loved Joe and admired how he was respected on the streets. My sisters spent most of their time in the house. But not me and Joe. My mother gave us freedom the girls could only imagine. I remember hanging around the neighborhood and seeing how boys and men reacted to Joe. My brother was an athlete; quite the runner. We used to practice together. It was never easy to keep up with him. I remember him being in plays in school and, for a brief moment, being somewhat normal. Then in a flash, that all changed. Joe became this character of sorts on the streets: chest puffed out with extra-base in his voice. When he moved or spoke people listened and responded. I liked that.

I wanted that. Why wouldn't I want power, respect, acceptance, and being seen as a leader? I was young but far from a fool. I learned from watching my brother that wearing your armor; the deep voice, and the puffed chest on the streets got you noticed so that's what I did. I tried to follow him everywhere he went but he would usually catch me and send me home. I did get some time with him and those times were fun. Some days it was us against others and other days it was us boxing it out with each other. We hung around the pool hall racking balls so much, Mr. Monroe would have us put on boxing gloves and box out our issues.

At times I caught the same hell people did in the streets from Joe but when I caught Joe's hell it was different. We had a relationship my mom and my sisters could never understand. Joe had problems on top of problems but I know now the one thing we had in common was needing to find a way to belong as boys and make sense of becoming men. The acceptance we got on the streets helped with the confusion and emptiness I felt. I think Joe must have felt the same way. I didn't know what I'm writing today was my truth back then but looking back, the moves and the choices we made were about being a part of something bigger than us. It wasn't long before I accepted whatever the street code was to feel supported and valuable, including popping valium and quaaludes.

Like any family, there is a culture and an understanding. There is common ground built upon the things we have in common. Sometimes the smallest things, the smallest pains in your heart and soul, can become magnets drawing you toward that same pain in someone else. I was drawn to my big brother and he was drawn to me even though he knew there was more inside me than he could ever allow himself to be. As I began sorting through my thoughts to write this chapter in *Seeds of Hope*, I realized how conflicted my brother must have felt. Here he was, a law-breaking screw-up, drawn to his little brother while knowing he had no control over where I was going and what I was becoming. To make things worse, my brother had enough love for me and self-awareness to throw out warning signs hoping I would listen more to his words than copy his actions.

His words never left me. I knew the trouble he led us to wasn't good. Still, in my mind, he wasn't all bad. Eventually, we would take turns being the leader in choosing the trouble of the moment. So much so that when we moved on Garfield Avenue, detectives came by looking for me because they suspected I was breaking into houses. They were right.

Joe hadn't been home long from jail when things changed forever. All I remember is a heated argument between Joe and my mother. Mom grabbed her pistol and fired shots and after that, Joe would never live at home again. I knew it. It was time for me to step up. I used to sit on the porch with a pistol to watch over my sisters. Serving others and putting people first was never something I did, it was always who I was, and who I am. The streets never changed that part of me although there would be other things life would change.

When Hope Began to Take Shape

The fact that my father was absent didn't mean there was no influence in my life. My mother was relentless. Hard-working, strategic, and all about getting results while getting it done. She was a firm, stern woman who saw things one way – her way. My mom had her hands full with raising seven children, growing professionally to provide for us, and making sure we had a foundation in God. I can remember the energy at church. As the pastor gave his sermon, it always got to the point where every word became one with the drums. Before long, it was full-on jumping and shouting. The room transformed. After a while, you knew who would lose it and just about when. I never got it. If I wasn't laughing with my friends and being threatened by my mother I was counting the minutes for the show to be over. What made things even more confusing was when I would see the pastor from the church around the neighborhood.

He was a different man when I saw him on the streets than when he was the hype man at church. Then one day I noticed a different church bus parked on the street in the neighborhood with white people getting out of it. I was surprised to see white people in our neighborhood and the fact that they had a church made me curious. I wanted to know more so I asked my mom about me going with some friends and she let me. When I walked through the door, I liked how it felt. This church was much calmer than ours. The pastor delivered the word; straight with no chaser. Of course, the music was different but it was more about the message than the music and the show.

Now, I was young and had no idea of how deep the message for the day was supposed to be. I did know why I felt more connected to this church than ours and it was because it felt real to me. I needed to be as close to what seemed real as possible. For all I did not know and for everything I still needed to learn, being a person who chose the closest thing to what was real is who I needed to be. I was blessed to be drawn to what was real and grew to be thankful I recognized it and listened to it early on. This gift would guide me and keep me through some of my darkest days up until this day.

I left church that day with a new way of seeing myself in the world and on those streets. Now, this didn't mean that I became a saint - far from it. Neighborhood people talk so the word traveled about me and Joe. Eventually, Uncle Lester stopped by the house to visit with an idea that would change my life: The Boys and Girls Club on 39th St. I had no clue the Boys and Girls Club existed so I didn't know what to expect. When we walked through the door, I was surprised to see a friend of mine playing basketball! There were games and all kinds of things to do. I remember thinking, *you can do all this here?* At that moment I had no doubt I wanted to be a part of this club and just like that, my uncle got me a membership. For the first time, something came before the streets. All I wanted to do was go to school and get through the day so I could go to the Boys and Girls Club after school. It wasn't long before football found me and I fell in love.

Defining Manhood on my Terms

It felt good to be good at something and appreciated for my talent. The acceptance I was looking for on the streets I got for playing football. Things were changing. My mother's boyfriend gave me a job at Boxley's Auto Repair sweeping up for fifteen dollars a week. I liked the money but my plan was never to like her boyfriend. I resented working for him since he wasn't my father. But in time, I grew to love him. That time in my life was one when my anxiety and fears were calmed. I was a beast on the field and the more I achieved the greater my confidence grew. I claimed going pro and playing for the Kansas City Chiefs. I had never felt better in my life and still, all I had gained and accomplished was not enough. My connections to the streets, my friends, the pills, and the drama of it all split me between two worlds. I still needed validation from them, to belong, and I liked shiny things.

By the time senior year began, I was off the football team because my addiction to pills and the street lifestyle had taken over. I managed to graduate even though I squandered the money my mother gave me to pay the graduation fees to walk across the stage. At that point, my mother made it clear that I was leaving her house if I didn't have a plan so I needed to get clear fast about what I was going to do with my life. I left the house on a walk. On that walk, I had time to think. I replayed everything I had gone through. I replayed everything I had done. I thought about who I chose to be and who I wanted to be. I came to the conclusion that who I wanted to be mattered more than what I had been settling for. I had to give myself a chance to do something different and that would never happen if I stayed in Kansas City. When I got back home, I was enlisted in the United States military.

That decision taught me something about myself. I learned that I am capable of choosing what works for me and being right about it. My addiction to pills was not based on me creating a habit by taking them. My addiction was more about needing what I was missing from that street community. The moment I decided to look to myself instead of others, I almost miraculously, had everything I needed. I cut those ties and everything associated with them and moved forward. I needed to know I could trust myself and something good could come from it. The military was an escape from one part of my life but I would continue to be faced with learning how to define and own who I wanted to be as a man.

While I was in the military at Fort Lewis Washington, I met a young woman and after a brief relationship she dropped by the barracks to let me know she was carrying our son. I did what I was raised to do so we got married. We didn't tell anyone so you can imagine how upset my mother was when she came to visit me in Tacoma, Washington, and I had a wife and son. Over time, we had three boys together before the marriage came apart. I was lost and still trying to connect to how to become who I wanted to be. I fell short and I felt like a loser because of it.

After the military, when I went to see what kind of work and assistance I could get, all they saw was a black man and assumed I was a deadbeat. Without proper guidance I was unable to find programs for me as a man. So I did all I knew how to do and that was run. I was not there for my children mostly because I had no clue how to be. That wounded little boy would plague the man. Eventually, I would have one more son and a daughter and more on my plate to juggle mentally, emotionally, and spiritually. It was time for me to choose to stay in my light. It was time to embrace my fears, my insecurities, my doubts, and my judgments.

I decided to own every inch of the ground I stood on to the best of my ability and to be content with my best being enough.

My Seed: Never Give Up

It took me time to see that I've always had favor in God's sight. For a long time, I let my mistakes define me. My mother was tough on all of us and in many ways, her disappointment about my choices haunted me. Just like I needed validation from Joe, the streets, football fans, just about anyone, I needed my mother to see more than when I fell short. Despite it all, I always found a way to keep pushing. I still made my share of mistakes. Maturity, however, showed me how to take what I struggle in and show others another way. Just because it's hard to do doesn't mean we don't see what to do.

When I look back over the years, I was always directed toward people who saw my light and wanted to pour into me. For a long time, I thought I was lucky to receive their knowledge and support. I thought, *wow I'm glad I was able to get what they had to give.* I never understood that I received and so did they. People who have a lot to give are intentional about who they share with because they are fed when they feed. I was chosen because I too have value. Their light was drawn to mine. Yes! I do have a light and it is my beacon to others just as theirs is to me.

I never would have learned this had I not chosen to move no matter what. At sixty-one years young, I feel like a newborn with a fresh mind, heart, and purpose. For the longest time, I felt like I didn't deserve what I wanted. I felt like the vision God put in my mind was above who I was. If I'm completely honest, at times, I still struggle with this. The difference today is that I know those feelings are a lie and the light I radiate is the only truth. I always tell my children two things. First, you're either in your light or you're not; there is no middle ground. The second thing is the way to success is a straight line. Insecurities, unforgiveness for yourself, doubt, and a lack of courage can take us off course. In the end, through successes and failures, when we keep moving, everything planted grows into something we can use. My seed has grown into a new way of seeing myself. I have witnessed God's glory. I am His greatest work. I always mattered. I've always deserved it. And now, I know it.

Delano Berry

Delano Berry born is a Kansas City Missouri native. Currently residing in Northern California, with his lovely wife, 5 boys and daughter. He's a proud grandfather, Army veteran, basketball coach and a sports official.

Delano's entrepreneurial spirit consists these days by empowering and protecting individuals, families and businesses with legal and identity theft solutions. His Love for cooking brings him into the kitchen. He maintains a rigorous workout routine and spends quality time with his family. He's and encourager of encourager. You can always find Delano encouraging others to put God first and stay in the Light of His way.

FAITH - THE SEED THAT GIVES ME HOPE

ROSCHEETA BRUNDIGE

Today is Friday, September 18th, 2020 and it has been a rough day.

Let's backtrack a little. I have been having some challenges during this 2020 year. Especially with the eye opening revelation that most of the things I feel I have missed out on in life is because of fear. After taking some time processing, praying, crying and what not, I decided to start to say yes to opportunities. Not many days after that decision I saw a Facebook post from Rochinda Pickens asking if anyone was interested in a collaboration. Well, I definitely was. I genuinely like Rochinda. She embodies a lot of things I need in my life. At the moment that I saw the post, I read it and quickly scrolled past it. Yep, I was interested and kept scrolling. Why? Fear.

Not two minutes later another author I know, Tia Crockett, asked for people to be featured in a book collaboration. Then the light bulb went off. That this was exactly the opportunity to look fear in the eye and say, 'not today' and say 'yes' to this opportunity. But I didn't, I just kept scrolling past. Why? Old habits die hard.

For the next day or so it bothered me then I decided to go for it. I went to look for Rochinda's post to get the instructions to participate and alas I couldn't find it. It was definitely a sign that I shouldn't sign up, right!? Did I wait too late and miss out on yet another opportunity. I was upset and mad at myself. I could just sit and stew in my anger and then get over it. That is what the old fearful Roscheeta would do. I had to reign all that in and push through. I decided to text her. Yeah, I personally know her and could ask her what to do. Why was I avoiding it? Fear. If I created an excuse that I didn't know what to do then it wouldn't be my fault I missed out? See what fear does.

She responded and it took me a day to send the email because I was battling that same fear again. Anyway the email was sent and she responded very quickly. I read the requirements and was excited, nervous and scared all at the same time. Then I read the phrase "pray on it...", I thought "Yeah, that's what I needed to do. Pray on it." I set a reminder in my phone for the day before the deadline to respond. Time passed and not one prayer was uttered about participation in the project. I did think about all the ways I wasn't qualified though. I thought about how my story wasn't inspiring. I thought about how I couldn't help anyone with their life's journey by sharing my life's journey.

In the meantime a friend of mine emailed me about a vending opportunity at her online event. She texted me to make sure I opened the email. I opened the email and read it and that was it. I didn't set a reminder to fill out the application and submit payment. I didn't reply to the text to say I was interested. I didn't even reply to say that I had read or received the email. Does this sound a little familiar? Actually that wasn't all of it. For the last week or so I've been saying that I need to send the money in and figure out how to do this virtual vending for the event. I was thinking and saying but not doing. Why? Because of fear.

So this morning my sister friend texted me to let me know that since I didn't mention being interested or reply to her text or email she gave my spot to another lady. She said she didn't remind me because she didn't want to pressure me, especially if I had other plans.

Insert gut punch, heartbreak, disappointment, anger, rejection and anxiety. I was in tears as I replied to her text basically saying, "It's ok. I should've written it down. Well, lesson learned. I need to move my feet..." yada yada yada. All the things that would make her think that I was ok.

But I'm not okay. I'm mad at myself. I hate that I defaulted to procrastination and I missed yet another opportunity. I hate it. Why do I default? Because of fear. Fear that I'm not good enough. Fear that I am not smart enough. Fear that if I don't have it all figured out then it's not for me and I am not worthy. I have the hardest time seeing myself as enough, worthy, etc.

Then I remembered the book collaboration deadline is tomorrow. I checked my calendar. Yes, it is tomorrow. I checked my email and read through all the things again. I came back to "pray about it". I bowed my head and asked the Lord to tell me what I should do. Silence and then memory (holy ghost) that I said I don't want to be like this. I don't want to live in fear and anxiety. I'm going to start saying yes to opportunities that scare me. So I replied to the email. and let's just say the rest is history.

I also had to take things into perspective. Giving people hope isn't about having a perfect life. It's about living out the hope that you have. The Psalmist said it best. "I would have fainted if I didn't believe to see the goodness of the Lord in the land of the living." Hope isn't about a destination but a determination to believe, strive and live for better. Hope is about not giving up. Hope is about perseverance. Hope is picking yourself up time and time again and striving for a better result. Hope is about walking without shame. Hope does not make you ashamed. So this is how I got here.

Now let's take this journey forward. This is why I have hope to overcome the spirit of fear and anxiety. I pray my hope builds your hope.

Why do I have hope to give? The Lord has shown me that I am not the same person I was thirty years ago, fifteen years ago, or even three years ago. He has shown me that as long as I am willing to learn and make small shifts in my life from the lessons of life that I can become a better person, a better sister, a better daughter. This hope came from the seed of faith.

My parents were saved when I was very young so I grew up in church. I watched as people were prayed for and were healed. I saw God transform the lives of people for the better. We were taught to pray and study the word of God. We attended every service and bible class. In my teenage years we met Pastor Johnny Kidd. He is one of the greatest bible teachers I've ever had. Over the decades of his teaching I learned to love the word of God and enjoy studying it. The word of God excites me. The word of God gives me hope. It gives me hope for a better future. As I learned about Abram and Sarai and how they did their own thing to try to bring about the promise of God which definitely was wrong, God yet kept his promise.

David slept with another man's wife and had the man killed and yet after repenting and suffering the consequences of his actions God still kept His promise. David is referred to as a man after God's own heart.

The apostle Paul was formerly known as Saul, the persecutor of Christians. He had an experience with God that had drastic consequences. But, once he was converted and obeyed God he became one of the greatest evangelists. He birthed multiple churches. He preached to the people that others thought were unworthy of redemption.

Ruth and Naomi were in a bad situation. In a land where without a husband or son life as a woman was dire. They were without money or protection. But God placed it on Naomi's heart to go home and as she returned home, Ruth married Boaz, a wealthy landowner, and they were taken care of and provided for.

Like these and so many others in the Bible you are not perfect, your life may have been horrific. You may have been traumatized, used and abused. You may feel worthless and think that God can't help you and your circumstances will never change. Let's not even go that far, let's just focus on this point here; God first wants your heart then he wants you to renew your mind. Once you begin to believe and think differently even if your circumstances don't drastically change, God will change you in those situations.

Young Daniel was taken into captivity but he refused to eat the king's meat and sweets and God blessed him to be stronger and wiser than the rest. Therefore, he obtained favor from the slave master. Older Daniel was delivered without leaving the lion's den. He sat with the lions and was not devoured.

Joseph was sold into slavery and he was put in prison. He used the gifts God gave him and he became second in command. He was still a slave, but he had power to save his family in time of famine.

God did this then and He will do it now. He is the same God. He has changed me from fearful and taking everything that the devil was throwing my way to a fearless soldier that is waging war against my enemy. He changed me from a fearful and timid child to a preacher of His gospel. He taught me to stand boldly. Even in my imperfections I have seen God change things to work in my favor. He has said that His strength is made perfect in weakness. We will never know how strong our God is unless we are too weak to handle what has come our way.

So I admonish you to pick up your faith again. Stand on hope again. Believe in God again. You can make it. You can overcome. You are a warrior. You are worthy. You are precious to God.

Roscheeta Brundige

Roscheeta Brundige experienced God at an early age. Through multiple and varied experiences, she has become a Sunday School teacher, a trained Missionary and an amazing Inspirational Speaker. She established *The Daily Shift* broadcast and a personal prayer ministry, through her Roscheeta Monique Brand.

Roscheeta's passion to encourage others to create a personal, spiritual walk has fueled her to create works to educate people. Through this prolific education, confidence is built through prayer, learning God's Word and having a Personal relationship with God for yourself.

Follow me at:
RoscheetaMonique.com
Facebook and Instagram at Roscheeta Monique

Twitter and Periscope:
RoscheetaMoniqu

Daily shift broadcast airs Monday thru Friday 7am-7:30am EST

THE VOICE WITHIN

Clarissa Knighten

"Why is there a goose egg on your forehead", I was asked? "I think a mosquito bit me", I replied. This is how a lot of mornings would start. My parents or our housekeeper would ask me this same question over and over. Looking around the room, the ceilings were as tall as mountains. Geckos would crawl across the walls. However, they are not harmful to humans, so they couldn't be an excuse. In the Philippines the weather was always tropical, fresh coconuts, pineapples and mangos in the yard. Nothing like the fruit in the grocery stores today, so I couldn't use that as an excuse for an allergic reaction. I played outside a lot so thinking a giant mosquito would bite me wasn't a big deal. Voila! ... The perfect cover up! Banging my head on the walls was a normal thing for me. "Make the voices STOP!" This phrase would repeat over and over in my head. It wasn't until we had moved back to the United States that I realized there was something drastically different between my siblings and me. Beyond the gap in age, I was different. I was the youngest of five. Being the youngest, your parents are either too tired to deal with you or forget you exist, or maybe, just maybe, the older children broke them in.

"Make the voices STOP", "I can't STOP crying", "Smile". People would say, "You have a beautiful smile", "You look angry when you don't SMILE." No one knew why I was crying. Direct quotes from all around me were embedded in my brain. Born in a state of "Hopelessness" from a little hole in the wall city in the northwestern corner of Arkansas, this little dark-skinned girl would continue feeding into the world standard until 2017. Before we get to 2017, let's discuss a few events that happened between the years of 1979 and 2017.

In 1979 I was 11 years old and my parents were divorcing. We were being up rooted yet again. This time there would no longer be tropical breezes and succulent exotic fruits and geckos thinking they were family pets. Now, I was living where there would be cold snowy days and I would be living among strangers. Can you imagine walking into a new school where all the faces staring back looked like you for the first time? "You talk funny", "you pimp when you walk". Pimp walk defined by the urban dictionary is a slightly controlled stagger on either the right or left leg that causes one to limp in such a way that it's noticeable to others. "I am pigeon toed!" I was referred to as the girl that pimps when she walks. There was one teacher however that recognized the plight of my path and allowed me to stay inside everyday remaining in class so I did not have to venture outside.

That teacher was Annie Frye, 5th grade teacher at Troost Elementary in Kansas City, Missouri. The first bulletin board I made together with her was one that I will never forget. It was an Easter bulletin board with huge bunny rabbits on it. She and I would chat. I was very fond of her, she was my protector and I definitely needed one. Soon as I began to open up to Ms. Frye, we had to move and I hated school again. Ms. Tinsley, uggg, my 6th grade teacher at John J. Pershing Elementary School was the extreme opposite of my 5th grade teacher whom I grew to adore. Boy did I hate that school. My new taunts, "Dang you are tall, are you sure you're 12?", "you pimp when you walk," here we go again. I had to endure more hurtful phrases. The girls didn't like me because I was developed and boys didn't like me because I wouldn't give them the time of day. The mosquitoes were far less in the midwestern United States, now only seasonal. How could I get away with banging my head and no mosquitos to blame? Voices are multiplying in my head causing my heart to race. Emotions are continuing to swell within my body.

Every new school was the same thing over and over as if a broken record had my name on it. Lincoln Prep Junior High and Lincoln High schools were the same. Each incident pushed me further and further inside the introverted fiber of my being. Was I ever going to get the help I needed?

Coach Jerry Price, my drafting teacher helped change my life by introducing me to the world of drafting and architecture. Coach Price was also coach over the track team. Although two of my four siblings were athletes I had zero interest. However, he pulled me in as the manager. In retrospect I think the job was made up to give me something to do.

By the time my sophomore year came around we were moving again. Seemed like life in the military still, although we weren't a military family at this time. This time unlike the others I had a choice of schools to attend; a local redneck school in Independence, Missouri or an uppity school in North Kansas City. North Kansas City wasn't bad, I didn't have a favorite teacher, but I was back in my environment. All white students and I could become invisible again. By my senior year I had started popping laxatives like candy and become a diehard Denise Austin fitness fan. This seemed like another way to mask depression and bulimia as it can be a mask itself in horrendous ways. Deep down I knew, hitting myself in the knees, wasn't normal. "Who does that crap?" All this time I knew Jesus understood. I knew He wanted a closer relationship with me. But I didn't really care. Life and the voices continued on. Causing self-harm only diverted me a few hours at a time now. Years would pass by and my family didn't know what to do. Surely, I should end my life and the pain would go away permanently. After two failed suicide attempts I am still here to share my story of *Seeds of Hope*.

The Seeds: while writing this chapter God showed me that everything happened in my life to bring me to this point. In 2017 after nineteen years in corporate America, a place where I gave my all, the model employee on all accounts; working late, giving up weekends because of my position, being a loyal employee. None of that matters when God gives you signs that it's time to move on. It happened first thing on a Monday morning in August. My position was outsourced. That's a fancy way of saying, "you are FIRED". I didn't want to leave when God showed me because of the "Golden Handcuffs" aka "great benefits". It was time to start a new journey and trust Him.

Isaiah 43:1-3 (New Life Version) But now the Lord Who made you, O Jacob, and He Who made you,- O Israel, says, "Do not be afraid. For I have bought you and made you free. I have called you by name. You are Mine! 2 When you pass through the waters, I will be with you. When you pass through the rivers, they will not flow over you. When you walk through the fire, you will not be burned. The fire will not destroy you. 3 For I am the Lord your God, the Holy One of Israel, Who saves you.

I was never quite sure why this bible verse became one of my favorites. How was I going to make it? I was divorced, an empty nester and without a job. I had to ask, God are you serious? You want me to do what? This time the voices in my head were real! YOU really want me to create my art full-time! These were questions that I didn't have the answers to. At some point the luxury of insurance, counseling, vacations, everything I was used to, would have to cease. A wise friend allowed me to cry, cry that ugly cry for about an hour then she ever so gently said. "What is the worst thing that could happen?" I had a fear of being homeless. "That will never happen. You could sell your home, stocks, and move in with family or friends. You will not be homeless". Jesus calmed the chaos of my world with words of comfort from this person and several people. He showed me that not a tear had fallen over the tumultuous situation that had occurred in my life. GOD has always spoken to me when I felt at my wit's end.

Hebrews 13:5 *(The Voice) Keep your lives free from the love of money, and be content with what you have because He has said, "I will never leave you; I will always be by your side."*

How do you figure out your coping strategies? Through countless hours of talk therapy. The first time I walked into a counselor's office the room was bright and full of soothing energy. It was strange walking into a new place and feeling comfortable immediately. Have you ever experienced an overwhelming comfort that made you cry? This is the same euphoric feeling I get when I relax and know that God is present. I recall journaling how I felt about my life being uprooted, like the way that I had lived with all of my life. Distinguishing reality from make believe could only happen when I received assistance from God, talk therapy, medication and understanding how my brain is wired. If people knew I took medication and struggled with depression would those in my circle or the world view me horrifically? It's taken years of self-work and being vulnerable to finally look at myself. That electric current that flows to sources we don't see is what my mind screams at times; over stimulation. Yet God still wants to use me for His glory even after I've turned my back on HIM so many times.

Through counseling I discovered another outlet for over stimulation. Opposite to self-mutilation, a challenge of finding other ways to cope was presented. Oh…. did I mention I had become sleep deprived due to constant nightmares. In the nightmares the house would always be different yet, the facts were always the same. With the help of talk therapy I was able to identify the root source; moving while growing up the majority of my life. It has its beauty and darkness. I also learned to sabotage every relationship I've had. When you move often you learn to not only build a high brick wall around yourself but you begin to distance yourself after a couple of years. This cycle can be exhausting until you learn how your individual physics work. Hands down I was a master of pushing people out of my life. I would be leaving them soon anyway or they would leave me, right? With my parents' divorce several states were added between my dad and me. All of these finite life details are what have given me a platform for my story. Speaking the transparent truth, my truth, while sharing the God given gift of creating wearable, sculptural art has helped me.

I've been able to openly discuss the victories in my life because of God's hand. *Seeing that speck of dirt that looks like a large grapefruit still rears its ugly head from time to time.* The difference is, when it is time to seek help God's hand is with me. Gratitude envelopes my entire being and continues to remind me that there is work yet to be done. If I am able to chat with one more person feeling alone, unaware where to start, desperately trying not to let people in and trying to stop the voices, I hear you and I want to help. This road has been laboring and rough for far too long. Keep looking for glimpses of beauty in the midst of life. Keep an open heart to hear God say:

Philippians 1:6 *(New International Version) being confident of this, that he who began a good work in you will carry it on to completion until the day of Christ Jesus.*

Today the only voices I hear are those of, "sharing my truth".

National Suicide Prevention Lifeline 1-800-273-8255

Clarissa Knighten

Clarissa Knighten is a designer in Kansas City, MO specializing in wearable art. Knighten left Corporate America in 2017 after 19 years to pursue her business, CEO of Rissa's Artistic Design, and a commercial model. As an artist, Knighten creates jewelry for the everyday person as well as expressionary bold pieces for the fashion runway and for gallery exhibitions. She founded Rissa's Artistic Design in 2007 as a way to navigate clinical depression. Part of Knighten's purpose behind Rissa's Artistic Design is to help people understand that they can use life's challenges to do something positive and impactful. Rissa's Artistic Design was birthed from counseling over depression and bulimia. She strongly feels that people have to remove the stigma surrounding mental illnesses. Amongst her many accolades, you will find Clarissa's work at the renowned The Nelson- Atkins Museum of Art, Kansas City Missouri as part of "Testimony" currently on exhibition.

WAVERING FAITH

Marla Henderson

H ave you ever been hit so hard it buckled your knees? Well I have. When it happened to me there was no one there to help me recover. I didn't know how this could be happening to me. I was told my life was in danger and there was nothing I could do about it. I was scared!

I was afraid to tell my husband of three years and my family. I needed to share this enormous fear with someone right away. My parents had moved from Kansas City, Missouri to a small town five miles outside Sedalia, Missouri. I had to find somebody to talk to. The only person who was not at work at the time was my big brother, Darrell. Now Darrell and I had the typical brother and sister relationship. He was older than I was and he never let me forget it. It wasn't until later, as we grew older that our relationship began to grow as siblings as well as friends. He just happened to be home that day. Trying to drive to his house, through the tears, still wrapping my head around my mortality I finally made it to my brother. When he opened the door and saw me standing there our eyes met, the tears began to flow like a waterfall. He tried to console me but I was distraught. We stood there and cried together. He allowed me to cry in his arms until I couldn't cry any more. It was difficult to explain what had happened to me. He knew it was bad. I was devastated. He was scared. I was scared!

I remember when I was a teenager I had always wondered what would happen if I got in a really bad accident and was disfigured. How would that impact my relationship with my new husband? Or worse, would my new husband hang around and support me? I had a nine month old son when this happened.

Now I'm thinking I'll be a single mother, because I just know, my new husband is not going to hang around when I share this with him. My husband and I dated for eight years before we married. We were too young to be talking about marriage. Neither had a pot to pee in, nor a window to throw it out. We wanted to be as sure as we could be that we could withstand anything together, including raising children together. I didn't want to have to do the life thing alone. He did hang around and he did take care of me and our son. He's a great man, a provider and he's my ride or die. So, to calm my fear of him leaving, he said, "Hey, I married you for better or for worse in sickness and in health until death do us part". You know what I did? Yep. The ugly cry.

I was working at MCI Telecom as a maintenance/installation technician. I was working with all men, most of them Christian men. I was the first woman, the first black person to ever work there. Now I had to try to explain to them what I had gone through. Everyone was more supportive than I could have ever imagined. But on this one dreaded day, it happened again. Just like the first time. There was nothing I could do except cry. And oh boy did I cry. I did the ugly cry, in front of all these men. My boss at the time, came to my desk and sat next to me and held my hand. Again, I tried to explain what I was experiencing and like last time, I couldn't. This was my job, a very good job. Not knowing if it would be in jeopardy or not, I sat there with my head down feeling ashamed that I was behaving this way, crying loud. My supervisor told me I could go home early if I needed to but I couldn't move. While I tried to figure out how to get my stuff together to leave, a coworker came in. As he was passing my desk he looked at me and said with no compassion at all, or so I thought, "what's wrong with you"? Frowning as he said it. He and I joked with each other all the time. I'm that person who has a great attitude and sense of humor. It had been put in one of my reviews that I had an *effervescent personality*. I was always in a good mood. So I was not surprised by his comment. He was like my work brother. We had great conversations about the Lord. He, unlike anyone else, started questioning me like I was on trial. The more he talked the worse I continued to feel. He knew this too, but he wouldn't stop. He simply asked me, "Have you given this attack on you to the Lord"? I couldn't speak after that. I never would have thought anything in this world could happen to make my faith waver.

You see, ever since I was ten years old, the first time I read in the Bible that if I had the "faith of a mustard seed nothing shall be impossible unto you". Matthew 17:20. I just have to have faith in Him. But my faith sure did waver on a cold March day in 1995. I am not proud of my lack of faith. Truth be told, my faith was all I had. I felt hopeless and alone. When my coworker said those words to me I cried and apologized to the Lord for not being strong in my faith and completely forgetting Him. Psalm 55:22 says, "cast your burden upon the Lord and he will sustain thee".

This was how I felt when I got the diagnosis Multiple Sclerosis for which there is no known cure. You could die from it. That was so hard to hear. It definitely felt like a hard kick and it did cause my knees to buckle. I had no choice but to give this diagnosis to the Lord, it was bigger than me. Let me explain what Multiple Sclerosis is. Multiple Sclerosis is an autoimmune disease that affects the central nervous system (CNS). The CNS controls the ability to walk and think. A disease in which the immune system eats away at the protective covering of the nerves which can cause nerve damage. Resulting nerve damage disrupts communication between the brain and the body.

At first, it seemed like I must have had every symptom you could have with MS. I experienced numbing so bad I couldn't tell if I had shoes on or not. I remember my mom and I had gone shopping one day and when we got to the store I got out of the car and started walking with her into the store and she happened to look down and said, "Where are your shoes"? I looked down and turned around and saw they were back at the car. I couldn't feel a thing. I could see the concern on her face. So, because I have such a good sense of humor, I said "Well looks like I'm going to have to buy tennis shoes that have the Velcro across the top like old people wear!" We both laughed and the concern on her face diminished. I lost my hearing in one ear. It sounded like what you might think ants sound like if they could talk. But with the other ear, I could hear just fine. Another symptom was my eyesight. It started doing something strange. I was driving to work and lost my vision but not completely, I had double vision. That was the most dangerous thing I'd ever encountered due to MS. God is good though. I made it to work safely and one of my coworkers had to bring me home. It seemed like it was one thing right after the other.

Once I was reminded by my work brother, "I can do all things through Christ who strengthens me". Philippians 4:13. I was good to go! My faith was back on track. It didn't go away. I was like the palm trees you see in a hurricane, they bend over to the point where you think the tree is going to break or snap then it doesn't. That was me and just like the palm tree, my roots, my faith was so deep a hurricane couldn't cause me to break away from my Heavenly Father ever again. No way! I had always studied the word since I was ten years old. My mom got me my first bible which I still have. Talk about planting a Seed of Hope. I would read that book for hours, not understanding most of it, but I held on to the words that I could understand. I wanted to please the Lord at that young age. I had a neighbor who lived up the street from me. She would invite me to go to church with her. She went to a Presbyterian Church. I loved that church. I learned so much there I became a member when I was nineteen or so. I'll say again, talk about planting a seed! So I've said all this to say, no matter what happens in our lives after knowing the truth, we should always, always, *always* put the Lord first. Trust in the Lord with all thine heart; and lean not unto thine own understanding (Proverbs 3:5).

I had asked the Lord why. Why did he allow me to contract such a debilitating disease? I remember being so incredibly angry at God and asking what did I do to deserve this? I had to fuss him out! After doing that, I did like I so often did, I went to the word. I opened up the book and read where Paul asked God three times to remove the thorn from his side. God said "my grace is sufficient for thee for my strength is made perfect in weakness "(2 Corinthians12: 9-10). Here I go again, screaming and crying the real ugly cry. I heard nothing back for a while. Several years went by, but my faith remained unwavering this time. "Those who hope in the Lord will renew their strength. They will soar like eagles; they will run and not grow weary, they will walk and not be faint" (Isaiah 40:3). I began spending much more time in the word regardless of how I was feeling, walking, seeing or hearing.

I knew God was with me. I started thinking less and less about my condition, which is what I started calling it, instead of a disease. I felt then like I had no more dis-ease. Get it? I felt great! Some years passed and the MS went into remission. It was in remission so long I had another child. The doctors at that time were against me having another child. So, doing my research and talking it over with the hubby we both decided to follow the doctor's recommendation. We had to figure out another way. Adoption! That was us figuring it out. But God had other plans. I had a daughter, my tiny little bundle of joy. She only weighed five pounds six ounces. We were able to raise our son and daughter together. But it wasn't until I gave this burden over to the Lord, that I felt the weight lifted. I thought if God allowed me to have MS, I must be able to endure it because he's with me. That gave me more strength. I laid this burden at his feet and left it there.

I was doing well until I fell down the stairs in my house, about eleven steps. I'll never forget, it was June 7th, 2007 on my fortieth birthday. My hubby was taking me to dinner that night and I was asking him what time we were going to be leaving. He was downstairs so I proceeded downstairs and slipped and fell. I was hurt. I was hurt so badly that on Monday morning I had to go to the doctor. I thank God I didn't break anything. The doctor did tell me it was going to take a while to heal. Because I was older. Really, forty is older? One thing I found out the hard way was, with MS if there is ever any trauma to the body it may cause an adverse reaction or what is called an exacerbation, in layman's terms a flare up or an episode. And it did just that, flared up. I walked with a limp from that day on. My walking got worse and worse. The MS was progressing. I had to go on disability. Another reason I have to praise the Lord. I filed for disability in December and got approved in April. I didn't need a disability lawyer like the commercials suggest. Although, I kept telling my husband I wasn't disabled because I was still doing everything. I even came up with a new word, definition and phrase. *diffrabled-* adjective; \ dif-fra-beld\ 1 A person or group of people living with a disability or an invisible illness who lead productive lives and are able to contribute and function in society. 2 A different kind of able.

I am still contributing to my household just in a different way. I might have to sit while cleaning out the fridge, or use a stool while cooking dinner. But I was still taking care of my family and business. I had to learn how to moderate and modify the way I do everything. As long as I do this I'm able to manage my condition.

As I've said before, I have a great sense of humor. God knew I would need it on this journey. I certainly thank him for that! My faith, still unwavered.

I did, however, start reading as much information about Multiple Sclerosis as I could get my hands on. That gave me power and strengthened my faith even more because as we all know, knowledge is power! I felt more confident in my new self. That's what I was, a new person, a different person. I had been transformed. When I was weak God was working on me making me stronger than before. He knew what was going to happen in my life and I would need to be stronger than ever.

Fast forward to February 2017. Now both of my children have gone away to college but not without having to take out parent loans. I had to get wise counsel from other family and friends on what I should do. Because I trusted my family and friends, I decided to take out the loans. Then one day I was home alone, and I got an unexpected call from an educational loan servicing company advising me they had received my information from the social security administration telling them I was disabled and may be in need of assistance regarding the loans I had taken out. Possibly eligible even having them forgiven. I was in such disbelief I couldn't contain myself. You know what I did, the SUPER UGLY CRY! All this time I couldn't understand how having MS would be a good thing for anyone. It was then that I realized why. Both of my children have been able to go to college. I will be able to help others with invisible illnesses and still keep a great sense of humor. So, I will drag a leg, use a cane or ride a scooter; whatever God says I need to do. I will witness about God's goodness and faithfulness forever. There's one thing I've learned - I don't know anything. I know God knows it all and if we keep our faith he'll lead us and sometimes even reveal some of the answers to the questions we ask him. Anyone with an invisible illness should remember, the Lord is with you always. Consider these seven steps:

1. If your attitude is not the best. Change it! Only you can do that.

2. Be gentle with yourself. It's ok to not be ok. We must put our pride aside.

3. Your attitude will truly affect your disease and how you handle it.

4. Don't stop! Keep doing what you can even if others say you can't.

5. Nutrition is huge. If you are unsure what you should be eating, ask your doctor for a dietitian's help. And take your vitamins!

6. Give yourself permission to grieve when you feel you've lost something or something seems to fade.

7. Connect with others who are in your similar situation.

Remember, stay grounded, keep your faith in the Lord, He is our source.

Glory and Thanks be to God!

Marla Henderson

Marla has spent her life as a vessel for the Lord's use. Calling Kansas City her home, she's the wife of Skip Henderson, for 30 years and mother of two adult children, EJ and Shelby Henderson. Marla's love for God, her family, and friends is what fuels her daily passion and gives her energy. She has a fun-loving, happy-go-lucky attitude type and has a great sense of humor. Marla loves to laugh.

A graduate of MIT (Missouri Institute of Technology)/DeVry. Her over 20 years-experience in telecommunications with at MCI/Worldcom has been instrumental in fueling path into education. Marla worked as substitute teacher in the Raytown School District, but after her diagnosis of MS (Multiple Sclerosis) she became extremely active in the MS community. Being one that has shifted her career over the years, she's known as a true leader in her community. She's a group Leader for MS Ray of Hope, MS Activist and a member of the MS KC council. Marla is a faithful member of Graceway Church where she serves on the dream team.

CROWNED KING BY THE KING

Trea Coleman

"Time to get up and get dressed, Trea. We don't want to be late for church", my great-grandmother would say early every Sunday morning. No matter what happened, my great-grandmother was going to make sure my brothers and I made it to church. The morning rush became as routine as getting to church and seeing all the elder women in their big colorful hats. Everyone greeted one another like they were family members related by blood. Our church was very small. But I learned the church wasn't about how many people were there. Instead, it was about taking time out for God and everyone who showed up was exactly where they should be.

Before long, everyone would head to their seats and, like many children, it was hard for me to sit still. My eyes scanned the room to see what other kids were doing while catching the breeze of the Martin Luther King Jr. paper stick fans. It is amazing how much you don't know you will remember later in life from those days in the church. One of my great-grandmothers' favorite quotes was, "Train a child up in the way they should go and when they are old, they will not depart." I heard her say this so much I could finish her sentence in my mind almost automatically. As a child, all I knew how to do was hear her quote. In time, life would present circumstances where her words would ring in my mind and replay on repeat. The difference became what I heard years ago I now knew how to listen to and apply when my mind replayed the message.

Those words my great-grandmother and our pastor spoke were imprinting themselves in my heart and stamping my soul. She knew I would need those words one day and with those words, she and God would always be with me. And, she was right. My brothers and I were loved and cared for. There was a community of strong God-fearing women who worked together to make sure we stayed out of trouble. I never liked trouble anyway. I had friends and other family members around me who had their fair share of run-ins with trouble; enough for me to learn why I didn't want that. One of the hardest things for me growing up was dealing with my anger. Although my father and I have a great relationship now, my father wasn't as active as I needed growing up. So whenever I saw my friends with their dads, I felt confused and sad. It never mattered what I was told or how it was explained to me. At the end of the day, all I wanted and needed was my dad and I didn't have him. At least I had my uncle for a short time. My uncle and I had a lot of fun together. We used to talk about sports and he would give me pointers on how to improve my game.

Through it all that, he still carved out space for me but when he had to leave it felt like a blow to my chest. Although I had the love and support of my great-grandmother and my church community, my uncle represented the safety and direction I needed from my father. My uncle spending time with me made me feel accepted and important. I had to get older to understand having my uncle around gave me a man to look to. He was my example of leadership. From seventh grade through high school was a difficult time for me because I had to try to figure everything I was feeling out on my own.

By the time I left home for college, I left with a few truths and some lies that would linger in my mind. One truth I knew was how much my family loved me and believed in me. One of many lies the Enemy made sure I replayed in my mind was that I was wasting my time by trying to better myself. Spending my childhood in the church would become the best thing my great-grandmother could have done for me. I would learn just how close I could bring God into my heart and circumstances whenever I chose to. I would learn the difference between using faith as a word and living faithfully because I believe God's words to be true. I would be tried, tested, and fail only to be tried, tested, and blessed for showing up in His name. God would show me who I was and why I was. God would take me through a transition to teach me how to own my position in my life and His kingdom.

The Real World

I was excited to be away at college. Now was the time for me to make my own decisions. I could wake up when I wanted, go to bed when I wanted, hang out as long as I wanted, and sleep as long as I wanted. I thought college life, my new life, would be easy. I mean, how hard can it be since I'll get to make my own choices? College life began very simply: I picked my classes, connected with my friends, planned to study, and collaborated on what we all would eat. Sure, the way I did things was different from home but things flowed well in the beginning. Until things got complicated. As the semesters went on, the expenses became more and more. There was only so much time in a day to work and still manage to stay on top of my classes and homework.

I didn't have a job and campus jobs with student pay weren't going to get me closer to closing the gap with the debt that continued to grow. It wasn't long before I couldn't help but feel the anxiety and stress from the weight of it all. The Enemy was never far. It was like those lies I had fought to forget the Enemy needed me to remember. As I sat in my apartment, I had to ask myself are these thoughts lies? Am I good enough? My father left so what does that mean? Am I smart enough? Worthy enough? Am I enough at all? I was scared, I felt alone, and I had pride. My pride wouldn't let me reach out for help. I didn't want the people who believed in me to think I couldn't do this. If they knew how I was struggling, they would worry and think college was too big for me. Or, if they knew would I think college was too big for me? I had to find a way out and letting people know I'm drowning couldn't be the way. See, I chose my truth and when that truth wasn't aligned with God, I opened the door for the Enemy to mix my truth with his lies. Together, the Enemy and I used the darkness in my life to create what seemed to be an instant fix. I decided to make the call to my friend and before I knew it, I had the drugs I needed to sell to make the money for tuition and bills.

And, that plan was working for a while. I was getting closer to solving my money problems and farther away from who I was raised to be. Those Sundays in the church were a part of me. I knew God could see me and that made me feel afraid. I knew better than what I was doing. More than that, I had turned my back on who I knew God created me to be. Just like my great-grandmother said, "Train a child up in the way they should go and when they are old, they will not depart". Pride and talking about faith while not moving based on my belief in the truth of His word was where I departed from what I was taught. My choices and feeling God's presence in the middle of my mess made me feel convicted. I knew I had to stop selling drugs immediately. After two weeks of job searching and being turned down, depression was setting in. I knew there had to be another way.

The fear, shame, doubt, and insecurity rushed into my mind and body. The sensation was overwhelming. I had to escape and find God. I heard my great-grandmother's voice in my mind saying, "go to your closet and pray". So one morning, I rolled out of bed, stepped into a closet, and got on my knees. I had never gone into the closet to pray before but what did I have to lose? I was tired of waking up day after day feeling depressed and worthless. I was tired of debating with myself about the truth of who I am. I was tired of being tired. So, while I was on my knees in that closet I got to air out the poison at the front of my mind. Then, I began to pray and I didn't hold back. I gave everything I feared, knew, didn't know, and wanted to know to God. The more I gave the closer I felt God near me. Before this day I was told God was real. On this day I knew He was real and He allowed me to feel His presence for myself. God listened to every word and calmed every concern. I went into that closet thinking I had nothing. I left that closet understanding I had everything I needed all along. I learned I always had faith but I didn't know how to activate it.

The moment I decided to humble myself to the possibility of His power and ask, I received. My problems in my life didn't go away instantly but my stress over needing to be my solution did. By the time I left that closet I felt like a two-ton boulder had been lifted off my shoulders. I also left that closet knowing that I could trust God to be my solution but in His own time; not mine. It turned out that God's time was two weeks from that day. I landed my dream job in human services and was able to pay for school out of pocket. More than my career taking shape, that time in the closet showed me the power of speaking up. Remaining silent and trying to figure things out in my head is the easiest way to be backed into a corner. God wanted more from me and soon I would learn what that meant.

Speaking Up

With my adult life and career taking shape, I wanted to share the journey with someone. Being alone did not feel like a good fit for me and I wanted success for myself. Success to me included having a wife and children. I wanted to be the father I always wanted for my children. I wanted to be a protector and support to my wife. So when I began dating, I immediately started playing my part in those relationships. In a previous relationship I experienced the baby daddy drama that came with a ready-made family. Of course, I could do without the drama but I chose to look beyond that drama. She wasn't all bad and in many ways, she needed me. I needed to be needed. The crazy part was I knew, in the beginning, all of the things I did not want for myself that would come with the relationship. Beyond the little white lies I would shrug off instead of speaking up, I began rationalizing why everything I disliked I should tolerate. To tolerate everything I disliked, I would stay silent and angry because silence gave me the escape I needed from addressing feelings I'd never acknowledged.

Even deeper, if I admitted to myself how angry I was in general, would I be ready to acknowledge what made me angry and why I ran from it? Before long, and a few more relationships, I chose to slow down and call on God for help once again. God revealed to me that I should pause and take a break from dating so I did. If I wanted to be a good husband to my future wife, I needed to become clear about who I was, what I wanted, and have the confidence to stand in that truth. I had to trust God will fill in all the rest. Not too long before this decision, my best friend passed away and I never took the time to grieve that loss. I felt lost and alone. Relationships were filling that void for me. When I decided to abstain from sex and practice self-discovery, God revealed to me some old wounds I needed to heal. I never felt protected and that made me feel unsafe. Feeling unprotected made me doubt myself and question my capability as a man. I was attracted to that same character trait in the women I dated.

I wanted to give to those women what I was still searching for myself. God taught me that there is a healthy way to protect and an unhealthy way to protect. I cannot give anyone, including the woman in my life, something I do not have. Choosing to humble myself to God during this time in my life brought me a feeling of peace and clarity I never knew possible. This time also taught me the power of allowing myself to share my truth. I learned I can trust myself to be myself and those who love me will understand and support me. Facing my fears and owning my voice led me back to my spiritual roots. I was all in. And then, there she was. I was so focused on God until I never saw her coming. My wife Andrea is that cool clean breeze after a soothing rain.

Her way is easy and free. Aside from being beautiful to look at, her intelligence and grounding in God sped up the pace of my heart. There was nothing she had to hide nor anything she needed to be for me or anyone else. She's just Andrea, a woman of God, and that's more than enough. She made me feel at ease; like I didn't need to wait for the little white lie. She was confident, secure, and supported. She was raised well and loved her family and friends. For the first time ever, I could feel the difference between being a protector to her in a healthy way versus being a protector to other women in an unhealthy way. Andrea was sent to me imperfectly whole and not in need of being fixed. The women before her came broken and needed me to help repair and sustain them. I thought *this is what love is supposed to feel like. This is exactly what I wanted.*

Meeting my wife let me know I was not destined to fail as a husband and father. I learned that just like her I am imperfectly whole in my own right. God sent her to me to complement and support me because I am worthy of being her protector. She has taught me so much. Most of all, she has taught me how to own my voice. My wife wants to hear what I have to say and creates a safe space for me to be heard. When I am with her I am reminded of how amazing God is and how much I matter to Him. God trusts me with Andrea and because of that, I am getting stronger in spirit every day. My seed of hope has always been faith. Now that I have grown in my faith I have learned that speaking on faith is not enough. I now know how to own my faith and I do that by allowing myself to become humble and go to God. When I go to God, I make sure I am open to receive His message and act on it. If you would like to own your faith, you must have that intention when you pray. If there is anything I want to leave you with it is to pray to God for vision, guidance, peace in times of uncertainty, wisdom, and to be kept through the journey. God is always wherever we need Him to be. All we need to do is believe when we call Him.

Trea Coleman

Trea Coleman is a native of DeKalb, Texas but currently lives in Dallas with his wife. Trea holds a Bachelor's degree in Human Services. Trea has several years of experience in the Insurance industry and currently acts as the principal of his own, Tax Service Business. The oldest of 7 siblings, Trea is a natural leader. As such, he's a proud member of Alpha Phi Alpha Fraternity, enjoys trading stock and crypto currency in his free time and traveling with his wife and friends. Trea's passion is fueled by understanding spiritual growth and using it as a compass through the different walks of his life. He's an avid reader, seeking to gain more knowledge to share and instill in those around him. Ultimately, his passion fuels him to fuel others.

NIA TAYLOR

"STREAKS OF GOLD"

The Bloodline

When I was a little girl, there was nothing more fascinating than the scalp of a doll's head. I would carefully follow the placement of every hair plug with my eyes and fingers. It all depended on the kind of doll, Barbie or an old school baby doll, what size the head would be and how much hair they would have, the density. Following the pattern of the hair plugs with my fingers while combing through the strands was captivating. I would have visions of all the different ways I could pull the strands to make that doll's hair look like the images I saw in my mind. Braiding was my favorite because the pattern braiding makes in hair could add or take away from a look. The feel of the hair between my fingers was exciting. I felt a sense of control. The power to make this doll's hair pretty was in my hands and I was up for the task. I didn't have time for pretend tea parties or outings with friends with my dolls. Nope. For me, the hair, and the way it felt, moved and smelled meant more to me than anything else. When I saw hair, I became curious and fixed on the possibilities. Yes, for me, hair was all about the passion that led to infinite possibilities and in time, I would learn why.

My love of hair continued to grow over the years. Of course, around the house, my grandmother used the pressing comb with the pressing cream to press my hair. I did not spend time at her salon when I was little, but in time I got the chance to be a part of that machine. My grandmother and grandfather both had their shops. My grandmother owned a very successful hair salon that was a staple in the community. This close-knit business was not only about transforming the look of women's hair, but it was about transforming and renewing the confidence of the women. Just the same, my grandfather owned a barbershop where men and boys of all ages came to get the crispest cuts in town. My lineage was in hair which is why I've always had a love affair with hair. The emotion I had in my chest was more than one thing. Yes, I loved the finished product-a flawless style. But more than the look, I learned my passion burned for how that look can become so much more for the client. The client experience, imagining with my doll that experience became the fuel for a passion passed down through my bloodline. Before long, I was practicing my skills with my friends in the neighborhood. My friend Chiquita is bi-racial. She has a thick curly texture of hair she let me practice braiding. It was challenging at first,- those strands and coils had a mind of their own. But the same detail I used when playing with my dolls, taking the time to feel each strand and follow the flow of the hair, I used with Chiquita.

Chiquita was like a walking advertisement for my work, and it took no time for other girls to ask me about braiding their hair. I spent a good portion of recess at school braiding my friend's hair. Most mothers don't like people in their daughter's hair, so my following was small yet big enough for me to perfect my technique and to realize I wanted to learn more.

As the years passed, the time finally came for me to learn more. The most exciting day of my life was when my grandmother told me I could come and work with her at the shop. I'll never forget what it was like when I walked through those doors. The atmosphere was like no other I'd experienced. There was so much to take in. The chatter from all the different conversations surrounding you made the voices resemble a buzz in the air. Stylists standing and working over their client's hair while other women waited under dryers. I was focused on the details many probably would have missed like the clicking of the curling and flat irons. Those sounds were like my own personal symphony. Let's not forget about all the different smells- the oils, shampoos, foams, hot irons, dryers, hot combs, relaxers, and hair elixirs. Shampoo girls were rinsing the hair, and towels being switched from the washer to the dryer. The phone rang from incoming calls and the occasional salesperson stopped by to see if the ladies were interested in buying that day.

Yes, this salon was fast-paced and on the move! This is what I had been missing all this time! I could not wait to get started. I started small, sweeping floors, and grabbing towels and promoted to shampooing and eventually roller setting. Before long before I knew I wanted a career in hair. I wanted to learn more and find my place in the industry. So, my journey continued, I continued to grow and in the year 2000, I became a licensed hairstylist.

Created to Shine, Refined to Reign

For ten years I serviced my clients and experienced the atmosphere of a few different salons. From the moment I began my professional career, I did not fit into the box the beauty industry tries to put stylists in. For one, I was a bold and beautiful plus-sized woman, and it became clear to me early on that I didn't fit the image of what many thought a stylist should be. I was dismissed and ignored by clients and other stylists. I have had clients schedule an appointment with me only to arrive at the salon, walk past me while I'm standing at the first chair, and ask another, thinner, stylist if she was me. When that stylist would answer "no" and point the client back in my direction, the look of disappointment on the client's face was something I had to work to overcome. I was never a part of the clique the stylists formed. There would be no after-work dinners or drinks. There would be no hanging out, no inside jokes to trade at work. I was never included in the culture of many salons. Not only did I lack the stereotypical look, but I had an eye for details and a unique skill set that was all my own. I was a rare commodity, and it would take time for me to learn this was meant for my good.

I was hired to work for a company called Beauty Brands which served stylists by keeping them booked with clients. The challenge with Beauty Brands was the clientele was predominantly white and I was not accustomed to working with Caucasian hair. To add to the learning curve, there were the awkward moments I experienced with clients. For example, when a client calls into Beauty Brands to be booked for a service, they are assigned the first available stylist on the schedule. When it was time, I would go to the front of the waiting area and call the name of the client assigned to me, typically a white woman. the client would approach me, look at me, and ask,

"Are you doing my hair?" I learned to shake off that feeling and do my job, but it was always an unpleasant situation

Because Beauty Brands had a retail floor as well, when I saw black women on the floor, I would walk up to them, hand them my card and say, "Hello, my name is Nia, and I was just letting you know I am here. Even if you're not looking for a stylist, please pass on my card." Before long, I had black clients calling in and booking with me which eliminated those awkward interactions.

For a short while, I was bothered, and I felt isolated from the culture of the salon. Here I am doing all I can to make others feel better about themselves when I struggle with feeling comfortable in my skin. I had allowed the opinions and judgments of others to be the ruler I used to measure my self-worth. But I knew better and doing better was what I had to figure out how to accomplish for myself. I decided that I was going to let go of wanting to be where "they" are. People have a right to choose what and who works for them and if I am not a part of what works, then that does not mean there is anything wrong with me. Maybe I don't fit into their world because God has a special space He designed for me and my tribe He has waiting for me to serve? Maybe. At the end of the day, I will never arrive at God's destination for my life if I stand still waiting on a seat in the vehicle He never sent to get me there. It was time for me to take my passion, talent, and peace forward. I needed to allow prayer, study, and the quest to grow despite it all to heal me on my journey forward.

Defining Success on My Terms

I knew it was time to make it a priority to offer a specialty service to an underserved population – those suffering from hair loss. I decided I wanted to become a certified Trichologist. Trichologists specialize in diseases or problems related to the hair and scalp. After doing some research, I learned about Connie Judge, the founder, and CEO of the National Trichology Training Institute (NTTI) in Stockbridge, Georgia. Little did I know, my decision to enroll in NTTI would make Connie and our class, trailblazers in Trichology. NTTI was special because it was the only Trichology training in the United States then and now. In addition to that, the institute was not only black-owned and operated but led by a black woman. In many ways, we all learned and grew together. When I enrolled in 2010, NTTI had not yet earned its accreditation. Connie had a vision, but she would have to execute that vision all while making sure our class received the highest quality education and training. In twelve months, we went from studying and trying to navigate coursework while a system for the program was being created around us to my being the first to receive certification from NTTI who, in that year, earned its accreditation. The victory for us all was so sweet, in many ways, because God ordered all our steps in living out our passions. At this space in my life, God continued to speak to me and guide me towards how He wanted to use me to serve others. God began to reveal to me what He saw in that little girl with a passion for hair so long ago. I began to see that God does not design any of us in His image to be caged. God is infinite, all-powerful, and abundant. This degree of greatness cannot thrive in any box. Therefore, I never fit in any box. God allowed me to see myself and my gifts the way He always had; good and very good. After all, my vision and passion for hair may have been in my blood at conception but the plan for my passion, the blueprint, was God's.

To find acceptance in my imperfect flesh was not a matter of validation from others who may or may not have their own opinion. Acceptance came for me when I embraced validation from the one who created every inch of this bold and beautifully talented woman in His image. I am because He saw fit to create me and that eventually became more than enough. But knowing and feeling is never enough with God. So, my next test was on the way. I decided to apply to the Hair Club For Men just after receiving my trichology certification when they had just one opening and I ended up getting the job. Not only was I the only black woman working at the Hair Club, but I ended up being the Treatment Specialist. My certification in trichology gave me an advantage no one else could match. During this time, the Hair Club sent me to Memphis to receive training on their techniques which helped me expand my knowledge and develop my process for my clients. This was a company experiencing success globally so God positioning me to be the Treatment Specialist means anyone who came through their doors saw me first, exactly what I needed for God to refine my gifts.

While I worked for Hair Club, I also maintained my booth at the salon, and Maggie, my esthetician, told me about an opportunity in Lee's Summit, a suburb of Kansas City, Missouri. I wanted an opportunity to work as a trichologist in a private room for my clients. I prayed for an opportunity where I could create an atmosphere and a private experience for my clients. I decided to walk by faith and apply for the opportunity. God saw fit for me to move forward and I was offered the position where I am today. Over the years, my goal was to own a salon of my own and for the longest time, I wondered why that hadn't happened for me. Then, I came to embrace what service in His name and for His glory truly meant. What I wanted for myself and the purpose of my creation God was trying to fulfill were two different things. I was born with many seeds and God watered them along the way.

Never Stop, Never Quit, and RISE

My seed of hope has been persistence. Because I was drawn to follow my passion, God led me where I needed to go. It's common to look for signs that God hears us. The signs God sent to me were like the brightest most golden streaks from the sun in the sky. It was because I never stopped and refused to quit, I rose, and I continue to rise. My coach told me that I don't brag about myself enough. At first, I couldn't see what she meant then I was taken back to my days of not fitting in. I quietly navigated that time while I worked. Maybe I've been quieter than I could be and should be for far too long. Sharing my story is a big step toward sharing my light in a way that is new and exciting and if I had chosen to stand still and wait until things felt better, I would not be where I am today. I am the rarest of commodities. I am uniquely relevant, necessary, and meant to thrive in God's anointing abundantly and so are you. My prayer is that the most difficult challenges you experience serve to remind you that the challenge exists to elevate you. The challenge is God's way of preparing you for His next task. The challenge is preparation and sharing your greatness allows God's validation of your worth to shine through. Know that your greatest triumph can be found just at the edge of your comfort zone and your only comfort will be in getting there.

Nia Taylor

My name is Nia Taylor. I am a beauty professional for over 20 years. In 2000 I became a licensed cosmetologist and have had the privilege to also gain my instructor's license along the way. In 2010 I became a certified Trichologist where I help assist people suffering from hair loss and scalp disorders. I am the owner of Streaks's of Gold Hair Restoration located in Lee's Summit Mo. I am also the owner and founder of Trichology Hair Education Services Inc. It's a nonprofit organization that h.e.l.p.s. (hair education lifting people's spirit). My brand is "all things golden". I chose this because it a great representation of my lifestyle. No matter how many times it goes through the fire it comes out not pressed or shaken but rich and solid and not to mention it never looses its value. I like to consider my life as valuable because I change lives through lifting people's self esteem daily. I love my life like it's golden!

LET'S DIG DEEP

This section of the book is designed for you to go a little deeper in your personal journey taking cues from the stories that have come before you. Although each of us has a story to share and these Seeds of Hope have been theirs, we want you to explore within.

We have prepared questions for you to ponder and meditate on to draw out the seeds of your own hope for your life now and in the future. Enjoy this part! Embrace what's within as you discover who you want to bring forth. Let's Dig Deep!

Rooted

Have you identified your Seed(s) of Hope? Give your seed of Hope a name, call him or her out! Write a thank you note in the provided space.

_____

_____

_____

_____

_____

_____

_____

_____

_____

_____

_____

_____

_____

_____

_____

_____

_____

_____

_____

_____

_____

Make a list of some organizations that you can share your seed (s) of hope with to be a World Changer.

Write a review on Amazon of this book and post a picture on Facebook with book in hand and tag Rochinda Pickens.

Faith- Seed That Gives Me Hope

Look at a past struggle and compare how you felt in it then versus now.

Write down the issues of your current struggle and list your expectations of how it will be to overcome that struggle.

How does looking at the first comparison inspire hope for the second comparison to come to fruition.

The Voice Within

What was your childhood like?

Compile a list of people that have given you " Hope". Now, write a few sentences about their influence in your life.

How can you encourage those with mental illnesses?

Wavering Faith

Make a list of people that you will connect with that are experiencing similar situations as you.

Write down your favorite bible scriptures and meditate on them daily

Crowned by the King

Have you prayed for something and whole heartedly trusted God with what you prayed for? Write them down here.

What are you allowing the enemy to control and have an effect on your thoughts and feelings thus keeping you away from the promise God made to you?

_____

_____

_____

_____

_____

_____

_____

_____

_____

_____

_____

_____

_____

_____

_____

_____

_____

_____

_____

_____

_____

Are you ready to go in your closet of prayer and plant a seed of hope? If so, write down your prayers here.

Streaks of Gold

Why isn't it necessary to fit in and be accepted even if it's uncomfortable and you don't understand at the time?

Why does God allow you to go through so many steps to reach what you are destined for?

Journey in the Sun: In Purposed Ground

In what ways are you willing to take the bold step of faith and make a commitment to change that allows God to use your YES and propel you into the purposed ground He has for your life?

Read Romans 8:28. Now go back once more and read the section of the story about the blessing in the geckos. Think about a time in your life, when God took an unwelcoming situation and used it for your good? How does it make you feel knowing that all things work for the good of those who love the Lord and that there can be a blessing even in desolate situations?

Witness

It time to start documenting your Brilliance. What is that one thing that continues to showing up in your life over and over.

Write these words and repeat: I AM Enough

WRITE WITH
CHINDA & PURPOSE

MICHELLE GINES

Now it's time to *Write with Chinda & Purpose!* This section of the book is dedicated to helping you write your own story and book. We know that everyone has a book in them. It's true. It's also true that most people never do because either they're afraid, don't think they can or just flat out never even thought about it. But what we do know is that you are not like anybody else. If you've participated in or purchased this book because someone you know participated in it; you're no ordinadry man or woman. In fact, I venture to say, you're probably extraordinary in your own right and YOU know that you have a story inside of you.

With that, this section is dedicated to helping you get started writing your book. And when you do, there's a potential opportunity of YOU being one of the next author's featured in Chinda's Seed Series of Books. *The Seeds of Hope* is the first in the series to be followed by, in no particular order, *The Seeds of Joy, The Seeds of Faith, The Seeds of Love,* or *The Seeds of Deliverance.*

The books will be a true encouragement to every reader with every page. So, think about joining a list of new and not-so-new authors that are embarking on a journey of discovery within themselves, but sharing their experiences for the good of the world. Here's a little Snippet of what each of the forthcoming titles are all about, see below:

- **The Seeds of Love** - What seeds of Love can you share in your marriage that has forever changed your life.

- **The Seeds of Joy** - Joy is an inside job that illuminates outwardly. Let's embark on a journey together sharing experiences of pure Joy.

- **The Seeds of Deliverance** - Deliverance is "Freedom" Unleashing the strongholds to a newfound love.

- **The Seeds of Faith** - Faith is a Mustard Seed

Now, here's what you can do to potentially become one of the authors in one of these amazing books. It's 5 simple steps to get started.

- **Write your Story-** Use the Write with Chinda & Purpose section to craft your story. Start writing.

- **Submit your story** – Send via email to chindaandfriends@gmail.com, in the Subject Line: put I've Got My Seed with your name, city and state just like this. We will know you're serious. (i.e. I've Got My Seed- Michelle Brown from St. Louis, MO)

- **Pay your $125 submission fee (nonrefundable)** to CashApp: $ChindaandFriends and in the note put Seed and your name, just like this. We will confirm with a receipt. (Seed-Michelle Brown St. Louis, MO)

- ***We'll Review your Story***- Your Seed Story will be reviewed by our panel of authors, coaches and the publisher. We are looking for quality over quantity, so be sure to be clear, be sincere and be ready to put your best foot forward. Participation in the The Seed Series and any other publications with Chinda & Purpose requires your very best. It doesn't have to be perfect, but it does have to be meaningful and heartfelt. We have an expert team of editors, designers and content managers to assist you in making your story shine. So, get it written and submitted. (Disclaimer: Not all submissions will be selected for participation. You will be notified if your story has been selected via email).

- ***Publish your Story***- If you are one of the blessed recipients selected to participate in the next book, you will be notified via email with Next Steps.

We look forward to hearing from you and helping you share your story with the masses. Let's get started.

A StepbyStep Guide to Helping You Write Your Story

Story writing helps us learn to put our thoughts into order and use written language to communicate those ideas. You can enjoy the process of the story writing as you create your own story for this book.

Taking these first steps towards writing your story can be both a fun and challenging activity for you. By planning to write it, you learn to put your own thoughts in order and then use written language to communicate those ideas in a variety of ways.

It's helpful to structure your story from beginning to end is a great way to make the writing process a whole lot easier.

Let's begin Writing Your Story

Instructions: Pray for God's divine flow, grace and support before you pick up the pen. Let every word written be from His guidance and inspiration. In matters that were hard for you this will be a help to you. As you begin to open up and reveal your heart; emotions and feelings will come. We created space for you to use this section to really begin your writing process, use every line on the page. Feel free to grab another journal or steno pad if you run out of room for your ideas. When the ideas begin to flow, they will be hard to stop. It helps to pull your thoughts out of your head. Review what you've written down to aid you in penning your unique chapter with substance, grace and love for your sister who's waiting to read your story.

Now, let's write your story using these elements. Repeat this exercise until you have a good handle on your chapter.

Step 1:

Think of an idea and a corresponding scripture or quote.

A good place to start is by grabbing a few books you have at home and reading the back cover. Look at and think about what was this author trying to give you in this book, bible or devotional. It'll help you start thinking about what you want to say to your readers.

Think of an idea. Questions to Ponder. Write your answer in the space below.

What gets me started?

_____

_____

_____

_____

What keeps me going?

_____

_____

_____

_____

Do I influence others?

_____

_____

_____

_____

If so, _how_ do I influence others?

_____

_____

_____

_____

Here's some space to write down your Story ideas, quotes and/ or scriptures

Challenge: Write Down 10 Ideas Now. Go!

Step 2:

Character and Setting.

Now, think of yourself as a character in the setting of your life. Ask yourself who was I then? Or who am I now? Think of it in this way, the pivotal times in my life when your "Seed' was being defined. What was that story? What was it that you learned? What was it that taught you? What difference did it make in your life? You as the character, in the setting that brought you a 'Seed' Moment. Were you a child or an adult?

Character and Setting. Now, think of yourself as a character in the setting of your life.

Ask yourself who was I then?

_____

_____

_____

Or who am I now?

_____

_____

_____

What is your "Seed' story?

_____

_____

_____

What was it that you learned? What was it that taught you?

_____

_____

_____

What difference did it make in your life?

Were you a child or an adult?

Here's some space to write down your Story character ideas.

Challenge: Write Down 10 Ideas Now. Go!

Step 3:

The Beginning

All good children's stories have a beginning, middle and an end. How did it start for you? How did you get there? This is the place where you might pull on your roots of childhood, in school, at work, with friends or alone. You've got to go there to help lead others. Set your opening scene. Include what's special or different about you then or now?

The Beginning Questions to Ponder. Write your answers in the space below.

How did it start for you?

_____

_____

_____

How did you get there?

_____

_____

_____

Set your opening scene.

_____

_____

_____

What's special or different about you then or now?

_____

_____

_____

Here's some space to write down your Story beginning ideas.

Challenge: Write Down 5 Ideas Now. Go!

Step 4:

The Conflict

Should I stay or Should I go? My family vs. my spouse, my job, my life. When did you wrestle with moving forward or standing still? Unless a conflict is presented often we remain silent or in neutral. Did you have a conflict? If so, define it. And don't forget that the conflict could have been from within yourself. Ask yourself the questions and write down your answers. This will help you in crafting your story.

The Conflict Questions to Ponder. Write your answers in the space below.

What was the conflict? If so, define it.

_____

_____

Should I stay or Should I go?

_____

_____

My family vs. my spouse, my job, my life.

_____

_____

How did you know it was a conflict?

_____

_____

Here's some space to write down your Story Conflict ideas

Challenge: Write Down 10 Ideas Now. Go!

Step 5:

The Turning Point

The turning point is usually in the middle of our story and helps to make a story more interesting or in this case the reason there is a story to tell. What made the difference? When was the shift? How did you pivot? Did someone say something or did God say something? Remember what made you do something different.

The Turning Point. Questions to Ponder. Write your answers in the space below.

What made the difference?

When was the shift?

How did you pivot?

Did someone say something or did God say something?

Here's some space to write down your Story ideas, quotes and/ or scriptures

Challenge: Write Down 5 Ideas Now. Go!

Step 6:

The Resolution

A good story doesn't finish without a final resolution. What was your result? What has been the win? Was it worth it? What would've been the result if you hadn't made a change, shift or pivot? This is the place where you think about how different life would've been without this experience.

The Resolution. Questions to Ponder. Write your answers in the space below.

What was your result?

_____

_____

_____

What has been the win?

_____

_____

_____

Was it worth it?

_____

_____

_____

What would've been the result if you hadn't made a change, shift or pivot?

_____

_____

_____

Here's some space to write down your Story resolution ideas.

Challenge: Write Down 5 Ideas Now. Go!

Step 7

The End

Were you able to finally achieve something, or did you learn an important lesson as a result? This is where you wrap up your thoughts about your experience. But open the door to giving your fellow sister, daughter, friend, prayer partner and all readers the call to action they may need for their life. This will be the 'life application' component.

The End – Questions to Ponder. Write your answers in the spaces below.

Were you able to finally achieve something, or did you learn an important lesson?

_____

_____

_____

What was it?

_____

_____

Life application:

_____

_____

What can the reader do?

_____

_____

_____

What do you want to encourage the reader?

_____

_____

_____

Can you list 2 or 3 steps will it take?

_____

_____

_____

Here's some space to write down your Story Ending ideas.

Challenge: Write Down 5 Ideas Now. Go!

ROCHINDA PICKENS

Best- Selling Author| Life
Shift Coach| Speaker

Have you ever been in a space where you felt the walls closing in on you?

What about a space that has prompted you to start over immediately without a plan?

Many women have lost their joy & hope. As a Life Shift Coach & Speaker, Rochinda has broken through the barriers of starting over. She helps women choose to live life again while embracing their breakdown and prepare for the breakthrough.

It's no better time than to start now.......

Finding Joy in the Journey; Choosing to live intentionally.

Rochinda has gracefully coached hundreds of women from the stage at her annual Kept Woman of God conference. As a Visionary she always see the remarkable results in everyone.

  @rochindapickens
@chindaandfriends

  Chinda And Friends

The
SEEDS *of*
DELIVERANCE

A collaboration of stories
that uncovers the journey of
"DELIVERANCE".

ROCHINDA PICKENS

A collaboration of stories that
uncovers the journey of "FAITH".

The
SEEDS
Of FAITH

ROCHINDA PICKENS

The
SEEDS
Of
JOY

A collaboration of stories that
uncovers the journey of "JOY".

ROCHINDA PICKENS

A collaboration of stories that
uncovers the journey of *"LOVE"*.

The
SEEDS
Of
LOVE

ROCHINDA PICKENS

Made in the USA
Middletown, DE
25 June 2021